# sandy, snowy and sunny places

## look book

**BBC**

The Tweenies like finding out about different parts of the world. They like sandy, snowy and sunny places.

telly time

Jake enjoys playing in the sandpit. He makes sandcastles and imagines that he is in a desert. Max shows Jake a video all about the Sahara desert in Africa.

## Word time

| | |
|---|---|
| | camel |
| | oasis |
| | lizard |
| | dune |
| | palm tree |
| | sand viper |

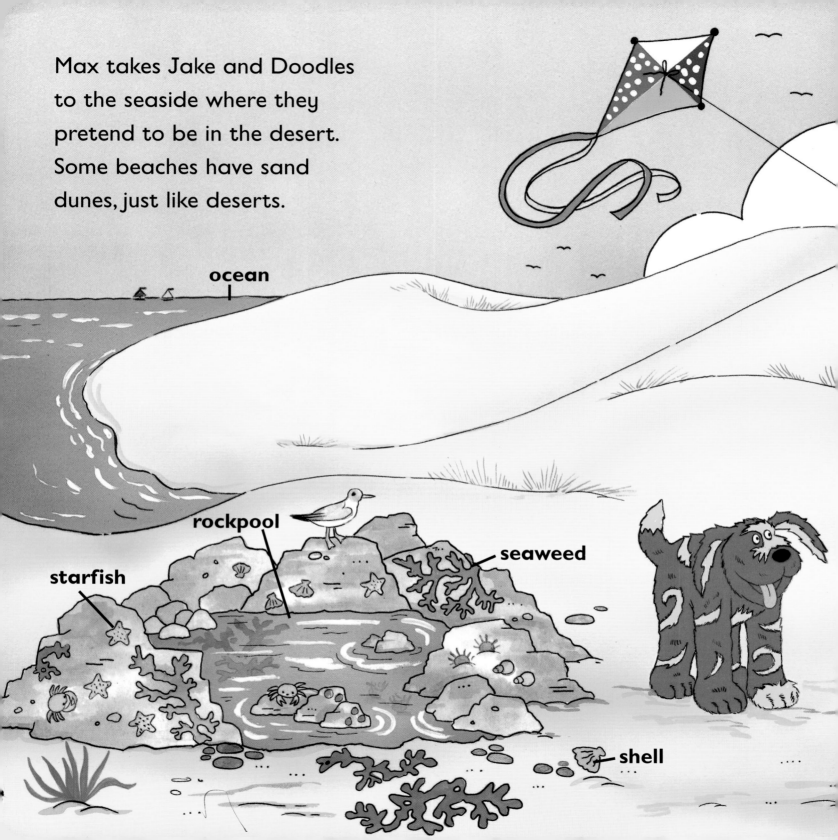

Max takes Jake and Doodles to the seaside where they pretend to be in the desert. Some beaches have sand dunes, just like deserts.

ocean

rockpool

seaweed

starfish

shell

seagull

dune

sand

Fizz likes tall trees and the pretty flowers that grow near them. Judy is showing Fizz a video about forests.

## Word time

fungi

flowers

trees

leaves

rabbit

Judy takes Fizz on a nature walk in the park. While they are walking, Fizz finds all the things on her list.

lake

ducks

rabbits

map

butterfly

bumblebee

picnic area

# Make your own tree

When Jake and Fizz get back, Jake makes a palm tree and Fizz makes an apple tree.

You will need:

apron

a long oblong of white paper or newspaper

sticky tape

round-ended scissors

paints and brushes

brown or red sheets of tissue paper

1) Roll the white paper into a tube. Stick the edges together with tape.

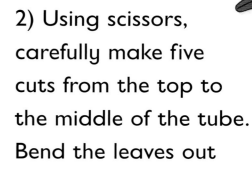

2) Using scissors, carefully make five cuts from the top to the middle of the tube. Bend the leaves out from the trunk.

3) Paint the leaves green and the trunk brown.

4) To make a palm tree, stick coconuts made from rolled up brown tissue in the leaves.

5) To make an apple tree, stick small pieces of red tissue onto the leaves.

telly time

Milo likes snowy, sandy and woody places, but most of all he likes water. Judy shows Milo a video all about places with water.

**Word time**

clouds

raindrops

river

waterfall

stream

sea

Judy takes Milo to see a waterfall. They watch the water flow into a river.

rain clouds

rainbow

meadow

river

waterfall

Bella likes snowy places,
especially when she can make
a snowman. Max shows Bella
a video about snowy places
around the world.

## Word time

sledge

huskies

snowmobile

iceberg

snowdrift

Max takes Bella to build a snowman. They give him a carrot nose, a hat and a warm scarf.

sledge

poles

goggles

ski slope

skis

# Make your own shaker

Bella and Milo are making shakers. Bella wants a snowy scene and Milo wants to make a watery shaker. Max shows them how.

You will need:

apron

a clean, small jam jar with a lid

small plastic figures to put in your shaker

waterproof glue

glitter

water

tape

1) Glue your plastic toy to the inside of the lid. Let it dry.

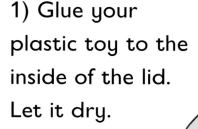

2) Pour lots of glitter into the jar.

3) Almost fill the jar with water.

4) Screw on the lid tightly. Use sticky tape to secure the lid. You might need a grown-up to help you.

5) Shake the jar.

The Tweenies have had a good time learning about sandy, snowy and sunny places. They have made palm trees, apple trees and shakers. What a busy time!